GEO-TECHNICAL ENGINEERING

AMAR KALYANE

Dedicated to...

My dear Wife & Daughter

Contents

Preface

This is the first edition, this Textbook is intended to present the currently accepted theories, design principles, and practices of geotechnical engineering. the assumptions and limitations used in developing a theory are pointed out and a sufficient number of examples and practice problems are included to illustrate the application of basic principles of practical problems.

Acknowledgements

At this ecstatic time of releasing the book. I, bow to almighty god for always keeping me under his shelter during this challenging phase of life.

I express my deep sense of gratitude to my parents for being a constant insiration for me and special thanks to my wife Sandhya for her keen observation on various aspect of the subject and help me in bringing out this book in an atrractive manner.

CHAPTER ONE

UNIT-I

INTRODUCTION AND INDEX PROPERTIES OF SOILS

Introduction to Soil Mechanics:

The term "**soil**" can have different meanings, depending upon the field in which it is considered.

To a **geologist**, it is the material in the relative thin zone of the Earth's surface within which roots occur, and which are formed as the products of past surface processes. The rest of the crust is grouped under the term "rock". To a **pedologist**, it is the substance existing on the surface, which supports plant life.

To an **engineer**, it is a material that can be:

- **Built on:** foundations of buildings, bridges.
- **Built in:** basements, culverts, tunnels.
- **Built with:** embankments, roads, dams.
- **Supported:** retaining walls.

Soil Mechanics is a discipline of Civil Engineering involving the study of soil, its behaviour and application as an engineering material. Soil Mechanics is the application of laws of mechanics and hydraulics to engineering problems dealing with sediments and other unconsolidated accumulations of solid particles, which are produced by the mechanical and chemical disintegration of rocks, regardless of whether or not they contain an admixture of organic constituents.

Soil consists of a multiphase aggregation of solid particles, water, and air. This fundamental composition gives rise to unique engineering properties, and the description of its mechanical behavior requires some of the most classic principles of engineering mechanics.

Engineers are concerned with soil's mechanical properties: permeability, stiffness, and strength. These depend primarily on the nature of the soil grains, the current stress, the water content and unit weight.

Formation of Soils

In the Earth's surface, rocks extend upto as much as 20 km depth. The major rock types are categorized as igneous, sedimentary, and metamorphic.

- **Igneous rocks:** formed from crystalline bodies of cooled magma.
- **Sedimentary rocks:** formed from layers of cemented sediments.
- **Metamorphic rocks:** formed by the alteration of existing rocks due to heat from igneous intrusions or pressure due to crustal movement.

Soils are formed from materials that have resulted from the disintegration of rocks by various processes of physical and chemical weathering. The nature and structure of a given soil depends on the processes and conditions that formed it:

- **Breakdown** of parent rock: weathering, decomposition, erosion.

- **Transportation** to site of final deposition: gravity, flowing water, ice, wind.
- **Environment** of final deposition: flood plain, river terrace, glacial moraine, lacustrine or marine.
- **Subsequent conditions** of loading and drainage: little or no surcharge, heavy surcharge due to ice or overlying deposits, change from saline to freshwater, leaching, contamination.

All soils originate, directly or indirectly, from different rock types.

Soil Types

Soils as they are found in different regions can be classified into two broad categories:

1. Residualsoils
2. **Transported soils**

Residual Soils

Residual soils are found at the same location where they have been formed. Generally, the depth of residual soils varies from 5 to 20 m.

Transported Soils

Weathered rock materials can be moved from their original site to new locations by one or more of the transportation agencies to form transported soils. Transported soils are classified based on the mode of transportation and the final deposition environment.

a. Soils that are carried and deposited by rivers are called **alluvial deposits.**

a. Soils that are deposited by flowing water or surface runoff while entering a lake are called **lacustrine deposits.** Alternate layers are formed in different seasons depending on flow rate.

c. If the deposits are made by rivers in sea water, they are called **marine deposits.** Marine deposits contain both particulate material brought from the shore as well as organic remnants of marine life forms.

d. Melting of a glacier causes the deposition of all the materials scoured by it leading to formation of **glacial deposits.**

e. Soil particles carried by wind and subsequently deposited are known as **aeolian deposits.**

SOIL FORMATION AND SOIL TYPES

Soils are the fundamental resource supporting agriculture and forestry, as well as contributing to the aesthetics of a green planet. They are also a base from which minerals are extracted and to which solid wastes are disposed. In addition, soils act as a medium and filter for collection and movement of water. By supporting plant growth, soil becomes a major determinant of atmospheric composition and therefore earth's climate.

ORIGIN OF SOILS

Soils are formed by weathering of rocks due to mechanical disintegration or chemical decomposition. When a rock surface gets exposed to atmosphere for an appreciable time, it disintegrates or decomposes into small particles and thus the soils are formed.

FORMATION OF SOILS

Soils are formed either by (A) Physical Disintegration or (B) Chemical decomposition of rocks.

A. PHYSICAL DISINTEGRATION

Physical disintegration or mechanical weathering of rocks occurs due to the following physical processes:

1. Temperature changes

Different minerals of rocks have different coefficients of thermal expansion. Unequal expansion and contraction of these minerals occur due to temperature changes. When the stresses induced due to such changes are repeated many times, the particles get detached from the rocks and the soils are formed.

2. Wedging action of ice

Water in the pores and minute cracks of rocks gets frozen in very cold climates. As the volume of ice formed is more than that of water, expansion occurs. Rocks get broken into pieces when large stresses develop in the cracks due to wedging action of the ice formed.

3. Spreading of roots of plants

As the roots of trees and shrubs grow in the cracks and fissures of the rocks, forces act on the rocks. The segments of the rock are forced apart and disintegration of rocks occurs.

4. Abrasion

As water, wind and glaciers move over the surface of rock, abrasion and scouring takes place. It results in the formation of soils.

Note: In all the processes of physical disintegration, there is no change in the chemical composition. The soil formed has the properties of the parent rock. Coarse grained soils, such as gravel and sand, are formed by the process of physical disintegration.

B. CHEMICAL DECOMPOSITION

When chemical decomposition or chemical weathering of rocks takes place, original rock minerals are transformed into new minerals by chemical reactions. The soils formed do not have the properties of the parent rock. The following chemical processes generally occur in nature:

1. Hydration

In hydration, water combines with rock minerals and results in the formation of a new chemical compound. The chemical reaction causes a change in volume and decomposition of rock into small particles.

An example of hydration reaction that is taking place in soils is the hydrolysis of

SiO_2

SiO_2+ $2H_2$ O $Si(OH)_4$

2. Carbonation

It is a type of chemical decomposition in which carbon dioxide in the atmosphere combines with water to form carbonic acid. The carbonic acid reacts chemically with rocks and causes their decomposition.

The example for this type of is, that is taking place in sedimentary rocks which contain calcium carbonate.

3. Oxidation

Oxidation occurs when oxygen ions combine with minerals in rock. Oxidation results in decomposition of rocks. Oxidation of rocks is somewhat similar to rusting of steel.

4. Solution

Some of the rock minerals form a solution with water when they get dissolved in water. Chemical reaction takes place in the solution and the soils are formed.

5. Hydrolysis

It is a chemical process in which water gets dissociated into H^+ and OH^- ions. The hydrogen cations replace the metallic ions such as calcium, sodium and potassium in rock minerals and soils are formed with a new chemical composition.

Note: Chemical decomposition of rocks result in the formation of clay minerals. The clay minerals impart plastic properties of soils. Clayey soils are formed by chemical decomposition.

<u>TRANSPORTATION OF SOILS</u>

The soils formed at a place may be transported to other places by agents of transportation, such as water, ice, wind and gravity.

1. Water transported soils

Flowing water is one of the most important agents of transportation of soils. the size of the soil particles carried by water depends upon the velocity. The swift water can carry the particles of large size such as boulders and gravels. With a decrease in velocity, the coarser particles get deposited. The finer particles are carried further downstream and deposited when the velocity reduces. A delta is formed when the velocity slows down to almost zero at the confluence with a receiving body of still water such as lake, a sea or an ocean.

All types of soils carried and deposited by water are known as alluvial deposits. Deposits made in lakes are called lacustrine deposits. Marine deposits are formed when the following water carries soils to ocean or sea.

2. Wind transported soils

Soil particles are transported by winds. the particle size of the soil depends on the velocity of wind. The finer particles are carried far away from the place of the formation. Soil deposits by wind are known as Aeolian deposits.

Large sand dunes are formed by winds. Sand dunes occur in arid regions and on the lee ward side of the sea with sandy beaches.

Loess is a silt deposit made by wind. These deposits have low density and high compressibility. The bearing capacity of such soils is very low. The permeability in vertical direction is large.

3. Glacier- deposited soils

Glaciers are large masses of ice formed by the compaction of snow. As the glaciers grow and move, they carry with them soils varying in size from fine grained to huge boulders. Soils get mixed with ice and are transported far away from their original position.

BASIC BEFINITIONS

A soil mass consists of solid particles which form a porous structure. The voids in the soil mass may be filled with air, water or partly with water and partly with water. Soil is a three phase system in general.

VOLUMETRIC RELATIONSHIPS

Void Ratio

Void ratio is the volume of voids to the volume of solids. It is denoted by **'e'**

e=Vv/Vs It is expressed as a decimal.

Porosity

It is defined as the ratio of volume of voids to the total volume. It is denoted by **'n'**

n=Vv/V

It is generally expressed as a percentage

1/n=V/Vv= (Vv+vs)/Vv 1/n= 1+ (1/e) = (1+e)/e

n=e/ (1+e) (a)

1/e= (1/n)-1= (1-n)/n

e=n/ (1-n) (b)

In equations (a) and (b), the porosity should be expressed as a ratio and not percentage.

Degree of saturation

The degree of saturation is the ratio of the volume of water to the volume of voids. It is denoted by 'S'.

S=Vw/Vv

The degree of saturation generally expressed as a percentage. It is equal to zero when the soil is absolutely dry and 100% when the soil is fully saturated.

Percentage air voids

It is the ratio of volume of air to the total volume.

n_a= Va/V

It is also expressed as a percentage.

Air content

Air content is defined as the ratio of the volume of air to the volume of voids a_c= Va/Vv

Also,

Water content

n_a=n a_c

The water content (w) is defined as the ratio of the mass of water to the mass of soilids w= Mw/Ms

It is also known as the moisture content (m). It is expressed as a percentage but used as a decimal in computation.

VOLUME-MASS RELATIONSHIPS

1. **BULK MASS DENSITY**

The bulk mass density (ρ) is defined as the total mass (M) per unit volume (V)

$$\rho=M/V$$

2. DRY MASS DENSITY

The dry mass density (ρ_d) is defined as the mass of solids per unit total volume $\rho_d= Ms/V$

3. SATURATED MASS DENSITY

The saturated mass density (ρ_{sat}) is the bulk density of the soil when it is fully saturated

$\rho_{sat}= Msat/V$

4. SUBMERGED MASS DENSITY

When the soil exists below water, it is in a submerged condition. The submerged mass density (ρ') of the soil is defined as the submerged mass per unit total volume.

$\rho' = Msub/V$

5. MASS DENSITY OF SOLIDS

The mass density of solids (ρ_s) is equal to the ratio of the mass of solids to the volume of solids

$\rho_s=Ms/Vs$

VOLUME-WEIGHT RELATIONSHIPS

1. Bulk Unit Weight (γ)= W/V
2. Dry Unit Weight (γ_d) = Ws/V
3. Saturated Unit Weight (γ_{sat}) = Wsat/V
4. Submerged Unit Weight (γ_{sub} or γ') = Wsub/V
5. Unit Weight Of Soil Solids (γ_s) = Ws/Vs

SPECIFIC GRAVITY OF SOLIDS

The specific gravity of soil particles (G) is defined as the ratio of the mass of a given volume of solids to the mass of an equal volume of water at 4° C.

$G = \rho_s/\rho_w$

The mass density of water ρ_{wat} 4°C is 1gm/ml, 1000 kg/m^3 or 1 Mg/m^3

BASIC RELATIONSHIPS

Sl No

Relationship in mass density

Relationship in unit weight

1

$n = e/(1+e)$

$n = e/(1+e)$

2

$e = n/(1-n)$

$e = n/(1-n)$

3

$n_a = n\, a_c$

$n_a = n\, a_c$

4

$\rho = (G+Se)\rho_w/(1+e)$

$\gamma = (G+Se)\, \gamma_w/(1+e)$

5

$\rho_d = G\rho_w/(1+e)$

$\gamma_d = G\, \gamma_w/(1+e)$

6

$\rho_{sat} = (G+e)\rho_w/(1+e)$

$\gamma_{sat} = (G+e)\, \gamma_w/(1+e)$

7

$\rho' = (G-1)\rho_w/(1+e)$

$\gamma' = (G-1)\, \gamma_w/(1+e)$

8

$e = wG/s$

$e = wG/s$

9

$\rho_d = \rho/(1+w)$

$\gamma_d = \gamma\, /(1+w)$

10

$\rho_d = (1-na)G\, \rho_w/(1+wG)$

$\gamma_d = (1-na)G\, \gamma_w/(1+wG)$

WATER CONTENT DETERMINATION

The water content of the soil is an important parameter that controls its behaviour. It is a quantitative measure of the wetness of the soil mass. The water content of the soil can be determined by any one of the following methods

1. Oven drying method
2. Torsion balance method
3. Pycnometer method
4. Sand bath method
5. Alcohol method
6. Calcium carbide method
7. Radiation method

SPECIFIC GRAVITY DETERMINATION

The specific gravity of solid particles is determined in the laboratory using the following methods

1. Density bottle method
2. Pycnometer method
3. Measuring flask method
4. Gas jar method
5. Shrinkage limit method

MEASUREMENT OF MASS DENSITY

The following methods are generally used for the determination of mass density

1. Water displacement method
2. Submerged mass density method
3. Core cutter method
4. Sand replacement method
5. Water Balloon method
6. Radiation method

PARTICLE SIZE ANALYSIS

MECHANICAL ANALYSIS

The mechanical analysis, also known as particle size analysis, is a method of separation of soils in to different fractions based on particle size. It expresses quantitatively the proportions, by mass of various sizes of particles present in the soil. It is shown graphically in a particle size distribution curve.

The mechanical analysis is done in two stages

1. Sieve analysis
2. Sedimentation analysis

SIEVE ANALYSISIS

This test is meant for coarse grained soils (particle size greater than 75 microns) which can easily pass through a set of sieves. The sieves used are 80mm, 40mm, 20mm, 10mm, 4.75mm, 2mm, 1mm, 600μ, 425μ, 212μ, 150μ, 75μ. The selection of the required number of sieves is done to obtain a good particle size distribution curve. The sieves are stacked one over the other, with decreasing size from top to bottom. A lid or cover is placed at the top and a pan, which has no opening, is placed at the bottom. Sieve analysis includes dry sieve analysis and wet sieve analysis.

gravels-sands-fines

Fig: Set of IS Sieves

sieve set

Fig: Set of IS Sieves

Fig: Illustrates Sieve Analysis test procedure

Fig: Illustrates Sieve Analysis test procedure

The water content at which the soil changes from the liquid state to the plastic state is known as the liquid limit (LL, W_l)

Fig: Shows Liquid limit test apparatus

CHAPTER TWO

UNIT-II

PERMEABILITY, EFFECTIVE STRESS AND SEEPAGE THROUGHSOILS

PERMEABILITY OF SOILS:

The property of soil which permits flow of water through it is called the permeability. Permeability is a very important property of soil. It will affect the settlement of buildings, yield of wells, seepage through and below the earth structures. It controls the hydraulic ability of soil masses.

656.png

p1.png

DARCY'S LAW

The flow of free water through soil is governed y Darcy's law. In 1856, Darcy demonstrated experimentally that, for homogeneous soils, the velocity f flow is given by, **v=ki**

where,

k= coefficient of permeability i= hydraulic gradient

the above equation is known as Darcy's law. The discharge 'q' is obtained by multiplying the velocity f flow by the total cross sectional area of the soil (A) normal to the direction of flow. Thus

q=va= kiA

the coefficient of permeability is defined as the velocity of flow which would occur under unit hydraulic gradient. It has the dimensions of velocity. It is measured in mm/sec. cm/sec, m/sec or m/day.

PPT 2.png

DETERMINATION OF COEFFICIENT OF PERMEABILITY

LABORATORY METHODS

1. Constant head permeability test
2. Variable head permeability test FIELD METHODS

1. Pumping out tests
2. Pumping in tests INDIRECT METHODS

1. Computation from the particle size or its specific surface
2. computation from the consolidation test data

CAPILLARITY-PERMEABILITY TEST

CONSTANT HEAD PERMEABILITY TEST

k= qL/Ah

where,

q = discharge (water collected by time0 L = length of specimen

A = area of cross section h = head causing flow

VARIABLE HEAD PERMEABILITY TEST

k = 2.303 aL/At [log (h_1/ h_2)]

where,

a = area of cross section of stand pipe L = length of soil sample

A = area of cross section of soil sample t = time

h_1 = initial head h_2 = final head

FACTORS AFFECTING PERMEABILITY OF SOILS

1. Particle size
2. Structure of soil mass
3. Shape of particles
4. Void ratio
5. Properties of water
6. Degree of saturation
7. Adsorbed water
8. Impurities in water

PERMEABILITY OF STRATIFIED SOIL DEPOSITS

a. **Flow parallel to plane of stratification**

$k_h = (k_h)_1 \times H_1 + (k_h)_2 \times H_2 + \ldots\ldots + (k_h)_n \times H_n$
$\mathbf{H_1 + H_2 + \ldots\ldots\ldots + H_n}$

a. Flow normal to the plane of stratification kv = H1 + H2 + Hn

H1 + H2 + ...+Hn
$\mathbf{(k_v)_1\ (k_v)_2\ (k_v)_n}$

e.png

Fig: Illustrates coefficient of permeability(K)

Fig: Illustrates coefficient of permeability(K) ranges.

EFFECTIVE STESS PRINCIPLE

1. DEFINITION OF EFFECTIVE STRESS

Let us consider a prism of soil with cross sectional area A. The weight P of the soil prism is given by
P = Unit weight of soil x h x A
Where 'h' is the height of the prism and 'A' is the cross sectional area of the prism

2. IMPORTANCE OF EFFECTIVE STRESS

The effective stress controls the engineering properties of the soils. Compression and shear strength of the soil depends on effective stress.

Total stress = effective stress + pore water pressure Effective stress = Total stress- pore water pressure Pore water pressure= Unit weight of water x h

Pore water pressure is also known as neutral pressure or neutral stress

1. EFFECT OF WATER TABLE FLUCTUATIONS ON EFFECTIVE STRESS

Soil above the water table is assumed as wet and soil below the water table is saturated. The total stress is obtained by multiplying unit weight of each layer with its unit weight. Effective stress is obtained by subtracting the pore water pressure from the total stress.

2. EFFECTIVE STRESS IN A SOIL MASS UNDER HYDROSTATIC CONDITIONS
3. INCREASE IN EFFECTIVE STRESSES DUE TO SURCHARGE
4. EFFECTIVE STRESSES IN SOILS SATURATED BY CAPILLARY ACTION

SEEPAGE PRESSURE

As the water flows through the soil, it exerts a force on the soil. The force acts in the direction of flow in the case of isotropic soils. The force is known as the drag force or seepage force. The pressure induced in the soil is termed as seepage pressure.

CHAPTER THREE

UNIT-III

STRESS DISTRIBUTION

SOIL STRESS CAUSED BY EXTERNAL LOAD:

External Load Types

- Point Load
- Line Load
- Uniform Load

Stresses in soil from surface loads

The stresses within a semi-infinite, homogeneous, isotropic mass, with a linear stress- strain relationship, due to a point load on the surface, were determined by Boussinesq in 1885.

- The stresses due to surface loads distributed over a particular area can be obtained by integration from the point load solutions.

- The stresses at a point due to more than one surface load are obtained by superposition.

  Tegangan14

In practice, loads are not usually applied directly on the surface but the results for surface loading can be applied conservatively in problems concerning loads at a shallow depth.

Vertical Stress Increase with Depth:

- Allowable settlement, usually set by building codes, may control the allowable bearing capacity
- The vertical stress increase with depth must be determined to calculate the amount of settlement that a foundation may undergo
-
- In 1885, Boussinesq developed a mathematical relationship for vertical stress increase with depth inside a homogenous, elastic and isotropic material from point loads as follows:

Westergaard' s Theory of stress distribution:

- Westergaard developed a solution to determine distribution of stress due to point load in soils composed of thin layer of granular material that partially prevent lateral deformation of the soil.

Westergaard' s Theory of stress distribution:
Assumptions:

1. The soil is elastic and semi-infinite.

1. Soil is composed of numerous closely spaced horizontal layers of negligible thickness of an infinite rigid material.
2. The rigid material permits only the downward deformation of mass in which horizontal deformation is zero.

WESTERGAARD METHOD

PointLoad

s z=

P

z^2p é

1
æ *r* ö2 ù3/ 2

ê1+ 2ç z ÷ ú

ëê è ø úû
1-2n
2 - 2n
a =
Tegangan0009

BOUSSINESQ VS WESTERGAARD
Tegangan0010b

Tegangan0010c

Tegangan0012c

COMPACTION OF SOILS

Compaction means pressing of soil particles close to each other by mechanical methods. Air during compaction is expelled from the void space in the soil mass and therefore the mass density is increased. Compaction is done to improve the engineering properties of the soil. Compaction of soil is required for the construction of earth dams, canal embankments, highways, runways and many other structures.

STANDARD PROCTOR TEST

To assess the amount of compaction and water content required in the field, compaction tests are done on the same soil in the laboratory. The test provide a relationship between the water content and the dry density. The water content at which the maximum dry density is attained is obtained from the relationship provided by the tests. Proctor used a standard mould of 4 inches internal diameter and an effective height of 4.6 inches with a capacity of 1/30 cubic foot. The mould had a detachable base plate and a removable collar of 2 inches height at its top. The soil is compacted in the mould in 3 layers, each layer was given 25 blows of 5.5 pounds rammer filling through a height of 12 inches.IS: 2720 part VII recommends essentially the same specification as in Standard Proctor test, some minor modifications. The mould recommended is of 100mm diameter, 127.3 mm height and 1000ml capacity. The rammer recommended is of 2.6 kg mass with a free drop of 310mm and a face diameter of 50mm. The soil is compacted in three layers. The mould is fixed to the detachable base plate. The collar is of 60mm height.

Procedure

About 3kg of air dried soil is taken for the test. It is mixed with 8% water content and filled in the mould in three layers and giving 25 blows to each layer. The volume of the mould and mass of the compacted soil is taken. The bulk density is calculated from the observations. A representative sample is placed in the oven for determination of water content. The dry density id found out from the bulk density and water content. The same procedure is repeated by increasing the water content.

Compaction curve

Water content

A compaction curve is plotted between the water content as abscissa and the corresponding dry density as ordinate. It is observed that the dry density initially increases with an increase in water content till the maximum density is attained. With further increase in water content the dry density decreases. The water content corresponding to maximum dry density is known as the optimum water content (O.W.C) or the optimum moisture content (O.M.C).

At water content more than the optimum, the additional water reduces the dry density as it occupies the space that might have been occupied by the solid particles.

For given water content, theoretical maximum density is obtained corresponding to the condition when there are no air voids (degree of saturation is 100%). The theoretical maximum density is also known as saturated dry density. The line indicating theoretical maximum density can be plotted along with the compaction curve. It is known as the zero air void line.

MODIFIED PROCTOR TEST

The modified Proctor test was developed to represent heavier compaction than that in the standard Proctor test. The test is used to simulate field conditions where heavy rollers are used. The test was standardized by American association of State Highway Officials and is, therefore also known as modified AASHO test.

In this, the mould used is same as that in the Std Proctor test. However, the rammer used is much heavier and has a greater drop than that in the Std Proctor test. Its mass is 4.89 kg and the free drop is 450mm. The soil is compacted in five equal layers, each layer is given 25 blows. The compactive effort in modified Proctor test is 4.56 times greater than in the Std Proctor test. The rest of the procedure is same

FACTORS AFFECTING COMPACTION

Water Content

At low water content, the soil is stiff and offers more resistance to compaction. As the water content is increased, the soil particles get lubricated. The soil mass becomes more workable and the particles have closer packing. The dry density of the soil increases with an increase in the water content till the O.M.C is reached.

Amount of compaction

The increase in compactive effort will increase the dry density at lower water content to a certain extent.

1. Type of soil

The dry density achieved depends upon the type of soil. The O.M.C and dry density for different soils are different

2. Method of compaction

The dry density achieved depends on the method of compaction

EFFECT OF COMPACTION ON PROPERTIES OF SOILS

1. Soil Structure
2. Soils compacted at water content less than the optimum generally has a flocculated structure.
3. Soils compacted at water content more than the optimum usually has a dispersed structure.
4. Permeability
5. The permeability of a soil depends upon the size of voids.
6. The permeability of a soil decreases with an increase in water content on the dry side of optimum water content.
7. Swelling
8. Pore water pressure
9. Shrinkage
10. Compressibility
11. Stress-strain relationship
12. Shear strength

METHODS OF COMPACTION USED IN THE FIELD

Several methods are used in the field for compaction of soils. The choice of method will depend upon the soil type, the maximum dry density required and economic consideration. The commonly used methods are

1. Tampers
2. Rollers

The compaction depends upon the following factors

1. Contact pressure
2. Number of passes
3. Layer thickness
4. Speed of roller Types of rollers

1. Smooth-wheel rollers
2. Pneumatic tyred rollers
3. Sheep foot rollers Vibratory compactors

COMPACTION CONTROL

Compaction control is done by measuring the dry density and the water content of compacted soil in the field

1. Dry density:

The dry density is measured by core cutter method and sand replacement method

2. Water content:

For the measurement of water content, oven drying method, sand bath method, calcium carbide method etc are used. Proctor needle is also used for this.

CHAPTER FOUR

UNIT- IV

COMPRESSIBILITY AND CONSOLIDATION OF SOILS

When a soil mass is subjected to a compressive force, its volume decreases. The property of the soil due to which a decrease in volume occurs under compressive force is known as the compressibility of soil.

The water is squeezed out of the clay over a long time (due to low permeability of the clay).

The compression of soil can occur due to:

1. Compression of solid particles and water in the voids
2. Compression and expulsion of air in the voids
3. Expulsion of water in the voids

The compression of saturated soil under a steady static pressure is known as consolidation. It is entirely due to expulsion of water from the voids

INITIAL, PRIMARY AND SECONDARY CONSOLIDATION

Initial Consolidation:

When a load is applied to a partially saturated soil, a decrease in volume occurs due to expulsion and compression of air in the voids. A small decrease in volume occurs due to compression of solid particles. The reduction in volume of the soil just after the application of the load is known as initial consolidation or initial compression. For saturated soils, the initial consolidation is mainly due to compression of solid particles.

Primary Consolidation

After initial consolidation, further reduction in volume occurs due to expulsion of water from the voids. When a saturated soil is subjected to a pressure, initially all the applied pressure is taken up by water as an excess pore water pressure. A hydraulic gradient will develop and the water starts flowing out and a decrease in volume occurs. This reduction in volume is called as the primary consolidation of soil

Secondary Consolidation

The reduction in volume continues at a very slow rate even after the excess hydrostatic pressure developed by the applied pressure is fully dissipated and the primary consolidation is complete. The additional reduction in the volume is called as the secondary consolidation.

Fig: Shows Diaphragm piezometer

CHAPTER FIVE

UNIT-V

SHEARING STRENGTH OF SOILS

Shear strength may be defined as the resistance to shearing stresses and a consequent tendency for shear deformation.

Soil derives its shearing strength from the following

1. resistance due to interlocking of particles
2. frictional resistance between the individual soil grains
3. adhesion between soil particles or cohesion

Necessity of studying Shear Strength of soils:

- Soil failure usually occurs in the form of "shearing" along internal surface within the soil. **Shear Strength**
- Thus, structural strength is primarily a function of shear strength.
- The strength of a material is the greatest stress it can sustain.
- The safety of any geotechnical structure is dependent on the strength of the soil.
- If the soil fails, the structure founded on it can collapse

Thus shear strength is "The capacity of a material to resist the internal and external forces which slide past each other"

Significance of Shear Strength :

- Engineers must understand the nature of shearing resistance in order to analyze soil stability problems such as;
  - Bearing capacity
  - Slope stability
  - Lateral earth pressure on earth-retaining structure

Fig: Shear Failure under Foundation Load

Fig. Shear Failure

At failure, shear stress along the failure surface reaches the shear Thus shear strength of soil is "The capacity of a soil to resist the internal and external forces which slide past each other"

Shear Strength in Soils :

- The shear strength of a soil is its resistance to shearing stresses.
- It is a measure of the soil resistance to deformation by continuous displacement of its individual soil particles.
- Shear strength in soils depends primarily on interactions between particles.
- Shear failure occurs when the stresses between the particles are such that they slide or roll past each other

Components of shear strength of soils

Soil derives its shear strength from two sources: –

- Cohesion between particles (stress independent component)
- Cementation between sand grains.
- Electrostatic attraction between clay particles – Frictional resistance and interlocking between particles (stress dependent component)

Cohesion: Cohesion (C), is a measure of the forces that cement particles of soils

Internal Friction: Internal Friction angle (*f*), is the measure of the shear strength of soils due to friction.

Factors Influencing Shear Strength: The shearing strength, is affected by:

- Soil composition: mineralogy, grain size and grain size distribution, shape of particles, pore fluid type and content, ions on grain and in pore fluid.
- Initial state: State can be describe by terms such as: loose, dense, overconsolidated, normally consolidated, stiff, soft, etc.
- Structure: Refers to the arrangement of particles within the soil mass; the manner in which the particles are packed or distributed. Features such as layers, voids, pockets, cementation, etc, are part of the structure.

Mohr Circle of Stresses

In soil testing, cylindrical samples are commonly used in which radial and axial stresses act on principal planes. The vertical plane is usually the minor principal plane whereas the horizontal plane is the major principal plane. The radial stress (σ_r) is the minor principal stress (σ_3), and the axial stress (σ_a) is the major principal stress (σ_1).

https://nptel.ac.in/courses/105103097/web/chap9final/s2_clip_image001.gif

To visualise the normal and shear stresses acting on any plane within the soil sample, a graphical representation of stresses called the Mohr circle is obtained by plotting the principal stresses. The sign convention in the construction is to consider compressive stresses as positive and angles measured counter-clockwise also positive.

https://nptel.ac.in/courses/105103097/web/chap9final/s2_clip_image002.jpg

https://nptel.ac.in/courses/105103097/web/chap9final/s2_clip_image002_0000.gif

Draw a line inclined at angle θ with the horizontal through the pole of the Mohr circle so as to intersect the circle. The coordinates of the point of intersection are the normal and shear stresses acting on the plane, which is inclined at angle θ within the soil sample.

https://nptel.ac.in/courses/105103097/web/chap9final/s2_clip_image004.gif

Normal stress

Shear stress

https://nptel.ac.in/courses/105103097/web/chap9final/graphics/

https://nptel.ac.in/courses/105103097/web/chap9final/graphics/

https://nptel.ac.in/courses/105103097/web/chap9final/graphics/

s2_clip_image006.gif

eq4.gif

s2_clip_image008.gif

The plane inclined at an angle of to the horizontal has acting on it the maximum shear stress equal to and the normal stress on this plane is equal to .

The plane with the maximum ratio of shear stress to normal stress is inclined at an angle to the horizontal, where a is the slope of the line tangent to the Mohr circle and passing through the origin.

When the soil sample has failed, the shear stress on the failure plane defines the shear strength of the soil. Thus, it is necessary to identify the failure plane. Is it the plane on which the maximum shear stress acts, or is it the plane where the ratio of shear stresses to normal stress is the maximum?

For the present, it can be assumed that a failure plane exists and it is possible to apply principal stresses and measure them in the laboratory by conducting a triaxial test. Then, the Mohr circle of stress at failure for the sample can be drawn using the known values of the principal stresses.

If data from several tests, carried out on different samples upto failure is available, a series of Mohr circles can be plotted. It is convenient to show only the upper half of the Mohr circle. A line tangential to the Mohr circles can be drawn, and is called the Mohr- Coulomb failure envelope.

https://nptel.ac.in/courses/105103097/web/chap9final/s2_clip_image002_0001.jpg

If the stress condition for any other soil sample is represented by a Mohr circle that lies below the failure envelope, every plane within the sample experiences a shear stress which is smaller than the shear strength of the sample. Thus, the point of tangency of the envelope to the Mohr circle at failure gives a clue to the determination of the inclination of the failure plane. The orientation of the failure plane can be finally determined by the pole method.

https://nptel.ac.in/courses/105103097/web/chap9final/s2_clip_image002_0000.jpg

The Mohr-Coulomb failure criterion can be written as the equation for the line that represents the failure envelope. The general equation is

https://nptel.ac.in/courses/105103097/web/chap9final/graphics/eq2-1.gif

Where = shear stress on the failure plane

c = apparent cohesion

= normal stress on the failure plane

= angle of internal friction

The failure criterion can be expressed in terms of the relationship between the principal stresses. From the geometry of the Mohr circle,

https://nptel.ac.in/courses/105103097/web/chap9final/graphics/eq3-1.gif

https://nptel.ac.in/courses/105103097/web/chap9final/graphics/eq13-2.gif

https://nptel.ac.in/courses/105103097/web/chap9final/graphics/eq16-1.gif

Rearranging,

https://nptel.ac.in/courses/105103097/web/chap9final/s3_clip_image002.gif

where

MOHR'S CIRCLE

Otto Mohr, a German scientist deviced a graphical method for the determination of stresses on a plane inclined to the major principal planes. The graphical construction is known as Mohr's circle. In this method, the origin O is selected and the normal stresses are plotted along the horizontal axis and the shear stresses on the vertical axis.

C

H

σ 3
P
O
Major principal plane
(σ 1+ σ3)/2
F
D
Minor princip al plane
σ 1

To construct a Mohr circle, first mark major and minor principal stresses on X axis. Mark the centre point of that as C. A circle is drawn with c as centre and CF as radius. Each point on the circle gives the stresses σ and τ on a particular plane. The point E is known as the pole of the circle.

1. Mohr's circle can be drawn for stress system with principal planes inclined to co- ordinate axes
2. Stress system with vertical and horizontal planes are not the principal planes

MOHR-COULOMB THEORY

τ
σ
Failure envelope

The soil is a particulate material. The shear failure in soils is by slippage of particles due to shear stresses. According to Mohr, the failure is caused by a critical combination of normal and shear stresses. The soil fails when the shear stress on the failure plane at failure is a unique function of the normal stress acting on that plane. Since the shear stress of the failure plane is defined as the shear strength (s) the equation for that can be written as

S= f (σ)

The Mohr theory is concerned with the shear stress at failure plane at failure. A plot can be made between the shear stresses and the normal stress at failure. The curve defined by this is known as the failure envelope.

The shear strength of a soil at a point on a particular plane was expressed by Coulomb as a linear function of the normal stress on that plane as,

S= C + σ tan φ

In this C is equal to the intercept on Y axis and phi is the angle which the envelope make with X axis.

DIFFERENT TYPES OF SHEAR TESTS AND DRAINAGE CONDITIONS

The following tests are used to measure the shear strength of the soil

1. Direct shear test
2. Triaxial compression test
3. Unconfined compression test
4. Vane shear test

Depending upon the drainage conditions, there are three types of tests

- Unconsolidated-Undrained condition
- Consolidated - Undrained condition
- Consolidated-Drained condition

<u>DIRECT SHEAR TEST</u>

Apparatus:

The test is conducted in a soil specimen in a shear box which is split in to two halves along the horizontal plane at its middle. The size of the shear box is 60 x 60 x 50 mm. the box is divided horizontally such that the dividing plane passes through the centre. The two halves are held together by locking pins the box is also provided with gripper plates plain or perforated according to the testing conditions

https://nptel.ac.in/courses/105103097/web/chap9final/s3_clip_image002_0000.jpg

Test Procedure:

A soil specimen of size 60 x 60 x 25 mm is taken. It is placed in the direct shear box and compacted. The upper grid plate, porous stone and pressure pad is placed on the specimen. Normal load and shear load is be applied till failure

Presentation of results:

- Stress – strain curve
- Failure envelope
- Mohr's circle

Merits:

1. the sample preparation is easy
2. as the thickness of the sample is very less, the drainage is quick
3. it is ideally suited for conducting drained tests on cohesionless soils
4. the apparatus is relatively cheap

Demerits:

1. the stress conditions are known only at failure
2. the stress distribution on the failure plane is not uniform
3. the area of shear gradually decreases as the test progresses
4. the orientation of the failure plane is fixed
5. control of drainage conditions is very difficult
6. measurement of pore water pressure is not possible

Tests on sands and gravels can be performed quickly, and are usually performed dry as it is found that water does not significantly affect the drained strength. For clays, the rate of shearing must be chosen to prevent excess pore pressures building up.

As a vertical normal load is applied to the sample, shear stress is gradually applied horizontally, by causing the two halves of the box to move relative to each other. The shear load is measured together with the corresponding shear displacement. The change of thickness of the sample is also measured.

A number of samples of the soil are tested each under different vertical loads and the value of shear stress at failure is plotted against the normal stress for each test. Provided there is no excess pore water pressure in the soil, the total and effective stresses will be identical. From the stresses at failure, the failure envelope can be obtained.

TRIAXIAL COMPRESSION TEST

The triaxial test is carried out in a cell on a cylindrical soil sample having a length to diameter ratio of 2. The usual sizes are 76 mm x 38 mm and 100 mm x 50 mm. Three principal stresses are applied to the soil sample, out of which two are applied water pressure inside the confining cell and are equal. The third principal stress is applied by a loading ram through the top of the cell and is different to the other two principal stresses. A typical triaxial cell is shown.

https://nptel.ac.in/courses/105103097/web/chap9final/s4_clip_image002.jpg

The soil sample is placed inside a rubber sheath which is sealed to a top cap and bottom pedestal by rubber O-rings. For tests with pore pressure measurement, porous discs are placed at the bottom, and sometimes at the top of the specimen. Filter paper drains may be provided around the outside of the specimen in order to speed up the consolidation process. Pore pressure generated inside the specimen during testing can be measured by means of pressure transducers.

- It is used for the determination of shear characteristics of all types of soils under different drainage conditions. In this a cylindrical specimen is stressed under conditions of axial symmetry. In the first stage of the test, the specimen is subjected to an all round confining pressure on the sides, top and bottom.
- This stage is known as the consolidation stage. In the second stage of the test called shearing stage, an additional axial stress called deviator stress is applied on the top of the specimen through a ram. Thus the total stress in the axial direction at the time of shearing is equal to the confining stress plus the deviator stress.
- The vertical sides of the specimen are principal planes. The confining pressure is the minor principal stress. The sum of the confining stress and deviator stress is the major principal stress.

- Triaxial apparatus consists of a circular base with a central pedestal. The specimen is placed on the pedestal. The pedestal has one or two holes which are used in the drainage function or pore pressure measurement.
- A triaxial cell is placed to the base plate. It is a Perspex cylinder. There are three tie rods which support the cell. A central ram is there for applying axial stress. An air release valve and an oil release valve are attached to the cell. The apparatus also have special features like,

  - Mercury control system.
  - Pore water pressure measurement device.
  - Volume changes measure.

Triaxial test on cohesive soil

CU, UU and CD tests can be conducted on soil specimen. The specimen is placed in the pedestal inside a rubber membrane. The confining pressure and axial pressure is applied till failure.

Triaxial test on cohesion less soil

The procedure is same as that in the cohesive soil only the sample preparation is different. A metal former, a membrane and a funnel are used for the sample preparation.

Merits

1. There is complete control over the drainage conditions
2. Pore pressure changes and volumetric changes can be measured directly
3. The stress distribution in the failure plane is uniform
4. The specimen is free to fail on the weakest plane
5. The state of stress at all intermediate stages up to failure is known
6. The test is suitable for accurate research work

Demerits

1. The apparatus is elaborate, costly and bulky
2. The drained test takes a longer period as compared with that in a direct shear test
3. The strain condition in the specimen are not uniform
4. It is not possible to find out the cross sectional area of the specimen accurately under large strains
5. The test simulates only axi symmetric problems
6. The consolidation of the specimen in the test is isotropic whereas in the field, consolidation is generally anisotropic.

Computation of various parameters

1. Post consolidation dimensions $V_0 = Lo \text{ X } (\pi/4. Do^2)$

   $Do = [Vo/(\pi/4 \text{ X } Lo)]^{1/2}$

1. Cross sectional area during shearing stage $A= Ao/(1-\xi_1)$
2. Stresses

   Deviator stress=P/A Principal stresses
   $\sigma 1 = \sigma 3 + (\sigma 1 - \sigma 3)$

4. Compressive strength

   The deviator stress at failure is known as the compressive strength of soil
   Presentation of results of triaxial test

   - Stress-strain curves
   - Mohr envelopes in terms of total stress and effective stress

https://nptel.ac.in/courses/105103097/web/chap9final/s5_clip_image002.jpg UU Test

https://nptel.ac.in/courses/105103097/web/chap9final/graphics/4_clip_image002.gif

All Mohr circles for UU test plotted in terms of total stresses have the same diameter. The failure envelope is a horizontal straight line and hence

It can be represented by the equation:

https://nptel.ac.in/courses/105103097/web/chap9final/graphics/eq4.gif

CU & CD Tests

https://nptel.ac.in/courses/105103097/web/chap9final/s5_clip_image002_0000.jpg

For tests involving drainage in the first stage, when Mohr circles are plotted in terms of total stresses, the diameter increases with the confining pressure. The resulting failure envelope is an inclined line with an intercept on the vertical axis.

It is also observed that $C_{CU} \neq C_{CD}$ and $_{CU} \neq {}_{CD}$

It can be stated that for identical soil samples tested under different triaxial conditions of UU, CU and CD tests, the failure envelope is not unique.

Effective Stress Parameters

If the same triaxial test results of **UU, CU and CD tests** are plotted in terms of effective stresses taking into consideration the measured pore water pressures, it is observed that all the Mohr circles at failure are tangent to the same failure envelope, indicating that shear strength is a unique function of the effective stress on the failure plane.

https://nptel.ac.in/courses/105103097/web/chap9final/s6_clip_image002.jpg

This failure envelope is the shear strength envelope which may then be written as

https://nptel.ac.in/courses/105103097/web/chap9final/graphics/eq8-a.gif

Where c' = cohesion intercept in terms of effective stress

f' = angle of shearing resistance in terms of effective stress

https://nptel.ac.in/courses/105103097/web/chap9final/graphics/

The effective stress acting on the rupture plane at failure, is the shear stress on the same plane and is therefore the shear strength.

The relationship between the effective stresses on the failure plane is

https://nptel.ac.in/courses/105103097/web/chap9final/graphics/eq16-2.gif

eq10-a.gif

UNCONFINED COMPRESSION TEST

The unconfined compression test is a special form of triaxial test in which the confining pressure is zero. The test can be conducted only on clayey soils which can stand without confinement. There are two types of UCC machines machine with a spring and machine with a proving ring

A compressive force is applied to the specimen till failure. The compressive load can be measured using a proving ring.

Image result for unconfined compressive strength

Fig. Unconfined Compressive Strength Test

Presentation of results

In this test the minor principal stress is zero. The major principal stress is equal to the deviator stress. The Mohr circle can be drawn for stress conditions at failure.

Merits

1. The test is convenient, simple and quick

2. It is ideally suited for measuring the unconsolidated undrained shear strength of intact saturated clays
3. The sensitivity of the soil can be easily determined Demerits

1. The test cannot be conducted on fissured clays
2. The test may be misleading for soils of which the angle of shearing resistance is not zero.

VANE SHEAR TEST

The undrained strength of soft clays can be determined in a laboratory by vane shear test. The test can also be conducted in the field on the soil at the bottom of bore hole. The apparatus consists of a vertical steel rod having four thin stainless steel blades or vanes fixed at its bottom end. Height of the vane should be equal to twice the diameter. For conducting test in a laboratory, a specimen of dia 38mm and height 75mm is prepared and fixed to the base of the apparatus. The vane is slowly lowered in to the specimen till the top of the vane is at a depth of 10 to 20 mm below the top of the specimen. The readings of the strain indicator and torque indicator are taken

Shear strength $S= T/[\pi(D^2H_1/2 + D^3/12)]$ Where T =Torque applied

D = Diameter of vane H_1= Height of vane

Image result for vane shear test on soil

Fig. Laboratory Vane Shear Test

Merits

1. The test is simple and quick
2. It is ideally suited for determination of the in-situ undrained shear strength of non fissured, fully saturated clay
3. The test can be conveniently used to determine the sensitivity of the soil Demerits

1. The test cannot be conducted on the fissured clay or the clay containing silt or sand laminations
2. The test does not give accurate results when the failure envelope is not horizontal.

Stress- Strain Behavior of Sands

Sands are usually sheared under drained conditions as they have relatively higher permeability. This behaviour can be investigated in direct shear or triaxial tests. The two most important parameters governing their behaviour are the **relative density (I_D)** and the magnitude of the **effective stress (σ')**. The relative density is usually defined in percentage as

https://nptel.ac.in/courses/105103097/web/chap9final/mathtypeeqn14-1.gif

Where e_{max} and e_{min} are the maximum and minimum void ratios that can be determined from standard tests in the laboratory, and e is the current void ratio. This expression can be re-written in terms of dry density as

eqn14-1.gif

https://nptel.ac.in/courses/
105103097/web/chap9final/
mathtypeeq/eqn15-1.gif

where $\gamma_{dmax}$and $\gamma_{dmin}$are the maximum and minimum dry densities, and $\gamma_d$is the current dry density. Sand is generally referred to as dense if I_D> 65% and loose if < 35%.

The influence of relative density on the behaviour of saturated sand can be seen from the plots of CD tests performed at the **same effective confining stress.** There would be no induced pore water pressures existing in the samples.

https://nptel.ac.in/
courses/105103097/web/
chap9final/
s8_clip_image002.jpg

For the dense sand sample, the deviator stress reaches a peak at a low value of axial strain and then drops down, whereas for the loose sand sample, the deviator stress builds up gradually with axial strain. The behaviour of the medium sample is in between. The following observations can be made:

- All samples approach the same ultimate conditions of shear stress and void ratio, irrespective of the initial density. The denser sample attains higher peak angle of shearing resistance in between.

- Initially dense samples expand or dilate when sheared and initially loose samples compress.

Example 1: A UU test is carried out on a saturated normally consolidated clay sample at a confining pressure of 3 kg/cm^2.The deviator stress at failure is 1 kg/cm^2.

a. Determine its total stress strength parameters.
b. If another identical sample is tested at a confining pressure of 4 kg/cm^2, what will be the vertical axial stress at failure?

Sol.

https://nptel.ac.in/courses/105103097/web/chap9final/s9_clip_image001.gif

https://nptel.ac.in/courses/105103097/web/chap9final/mathtypeeq/eq121.gif

From the plot, note that $_{UU}$ = 0 and https://nptel.ac.in/courses/105103097/web/chap9final/mathtypeeq/eq122.gif

https://nptel.ac.in/courses/105103097/web/chap9final/mathtypeeq/eq124.gif

https://nptel.ac.in/courses/105103097/web/chap9final/mathtypeeq/eq125.gif

https://nptel.ac.in/courses/105103097/web/chap9final/mathtypeeq/eq126.gif

UU tests on identical samples yield the same failure deviator stress at all confining pressures. Therefore, the vertical axial stress at failure,

9 798887 176994

Printed by Libri Plureos GmbH in Hamburg,
Germany